BULLSHIT

SWEAR WORD COLORING BOOK

The Universe Adult Coloring Book
featured with beautiful geometry

By

Florence Clark

Happy Coloring!

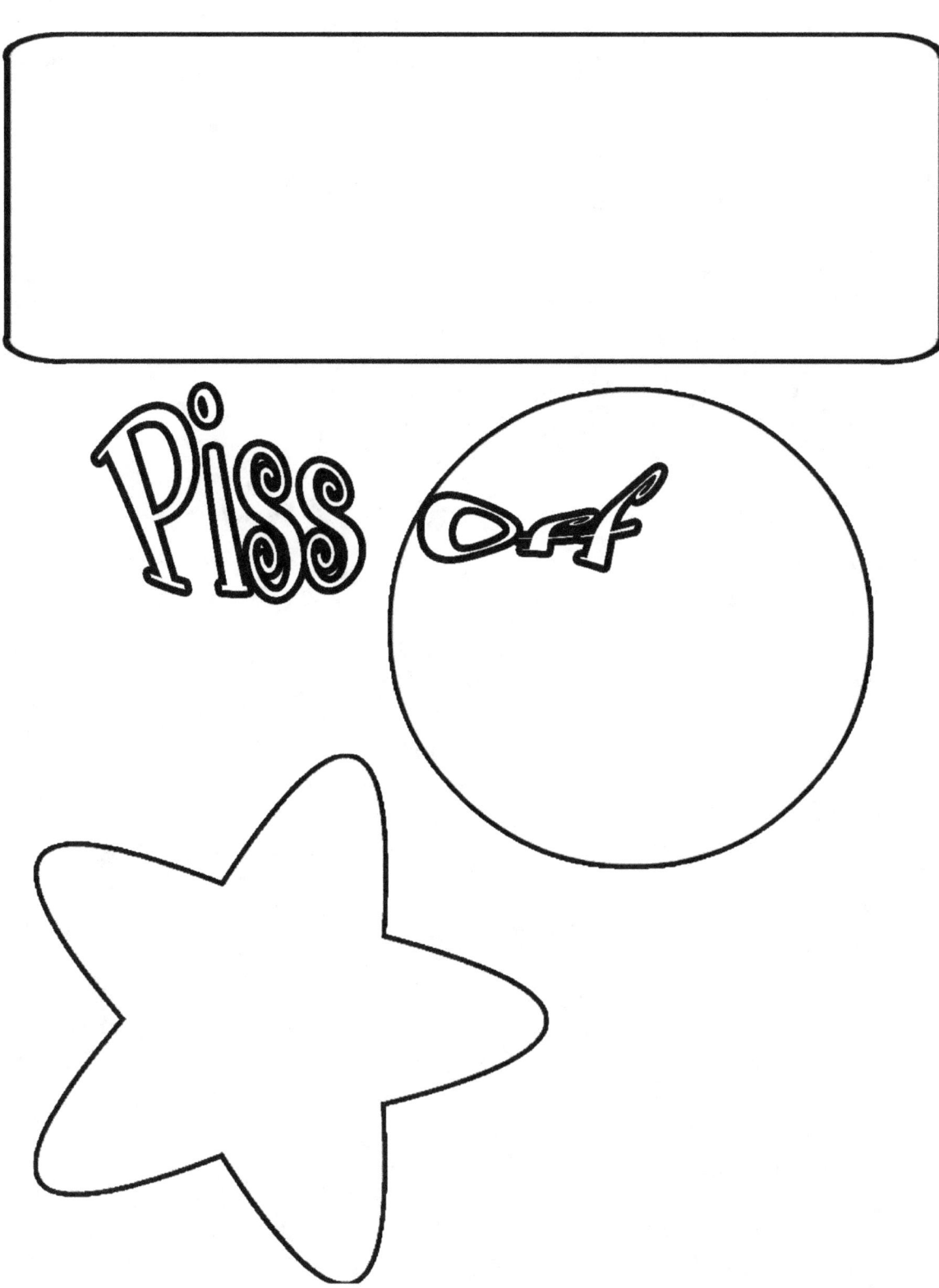

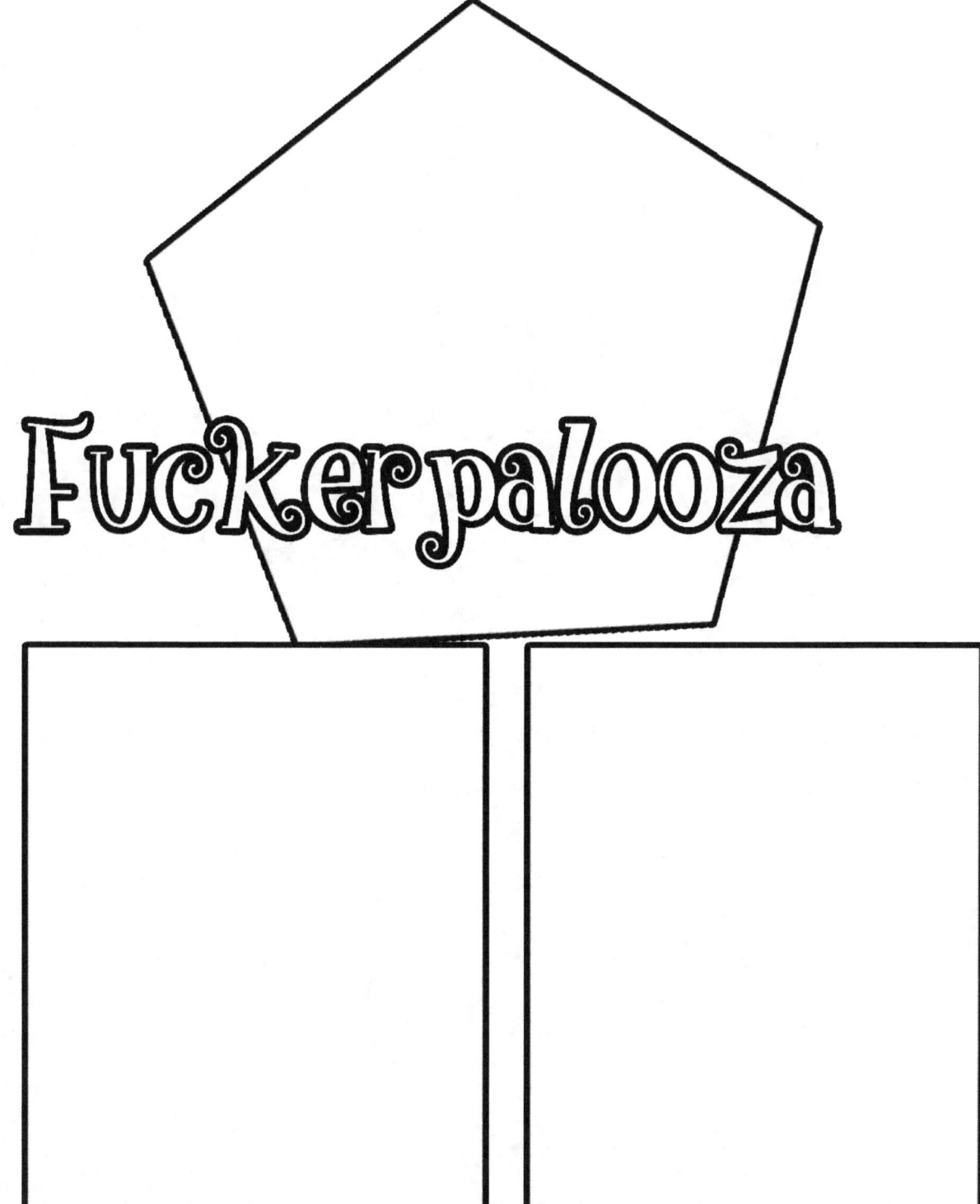

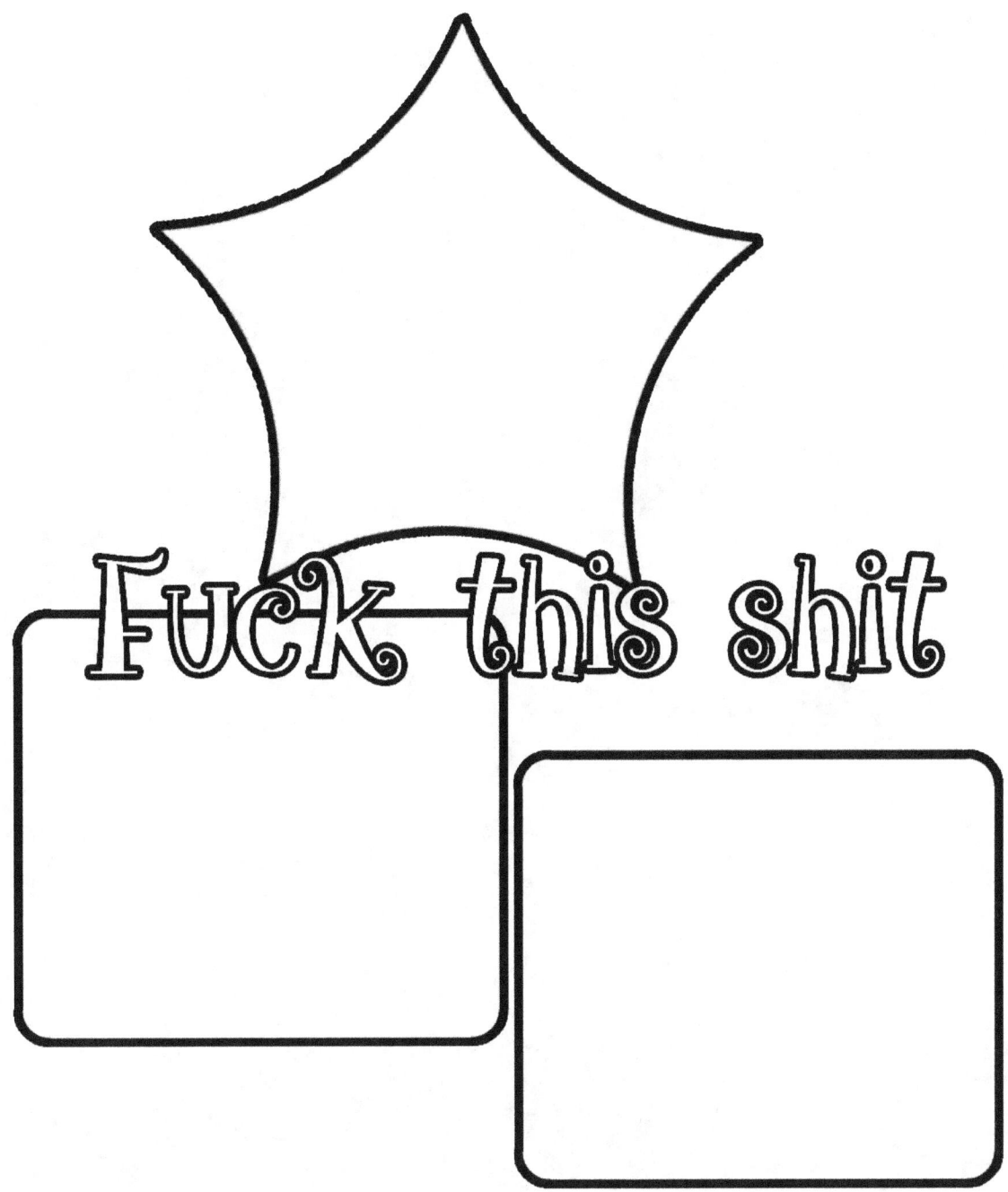

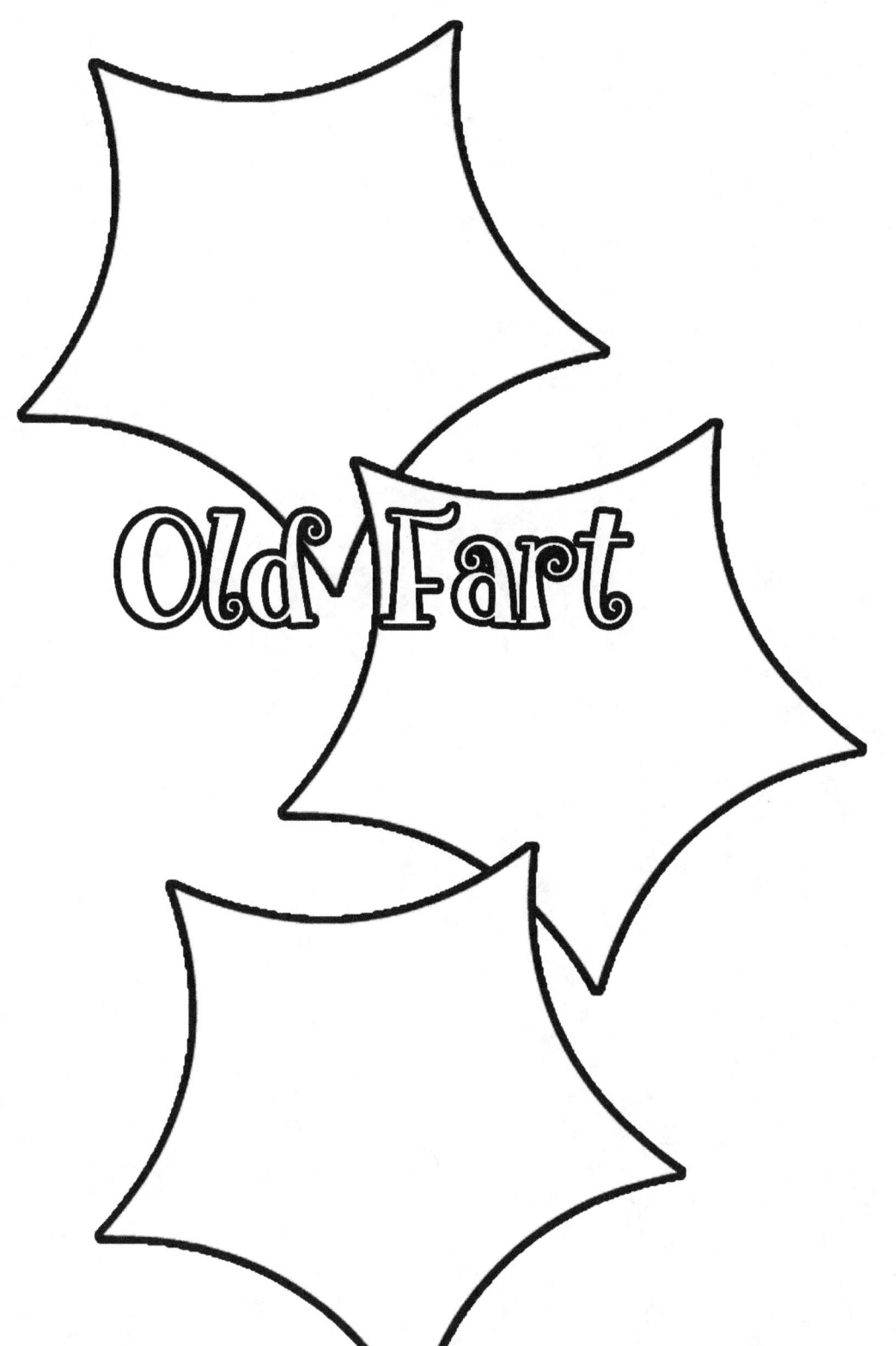

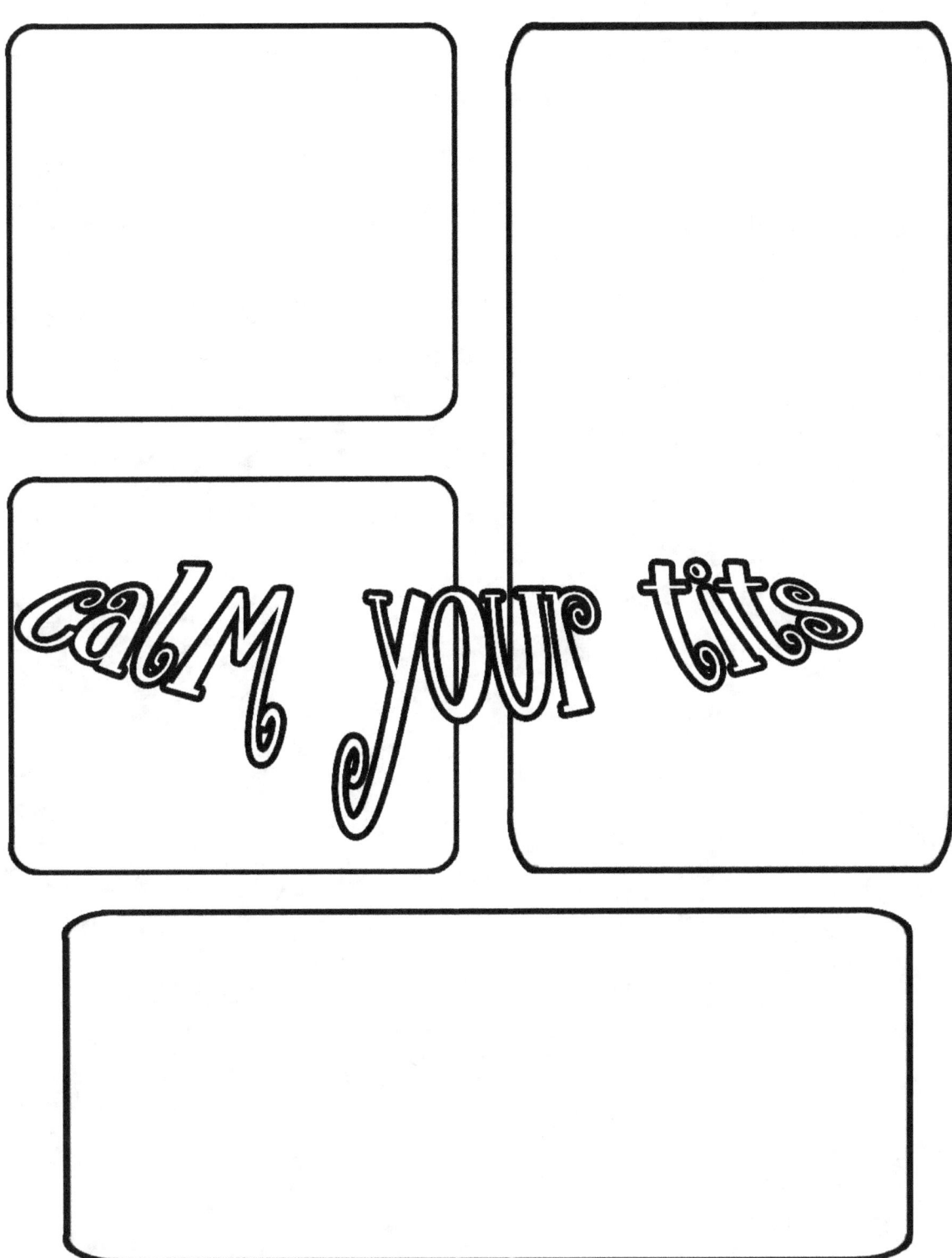

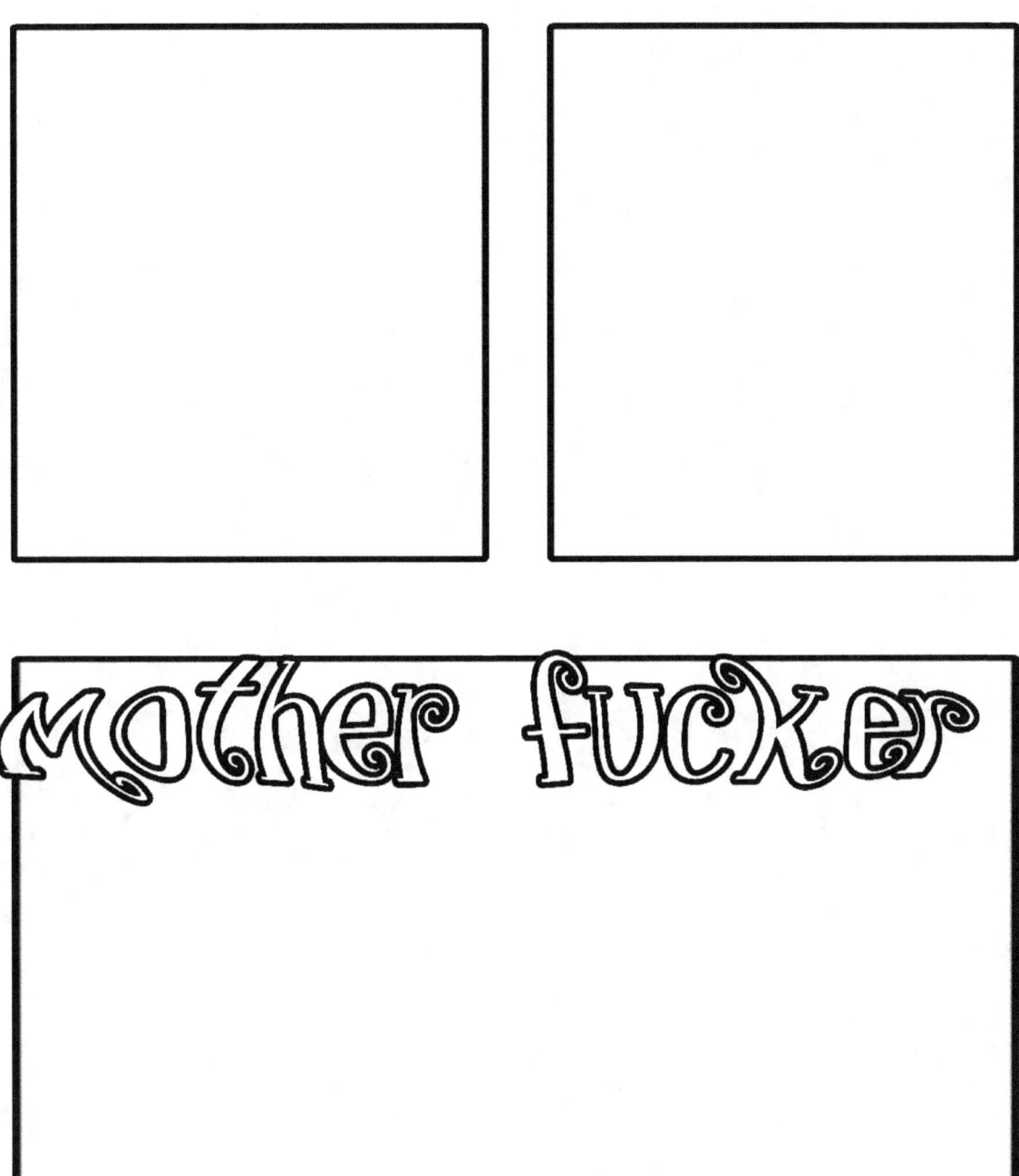

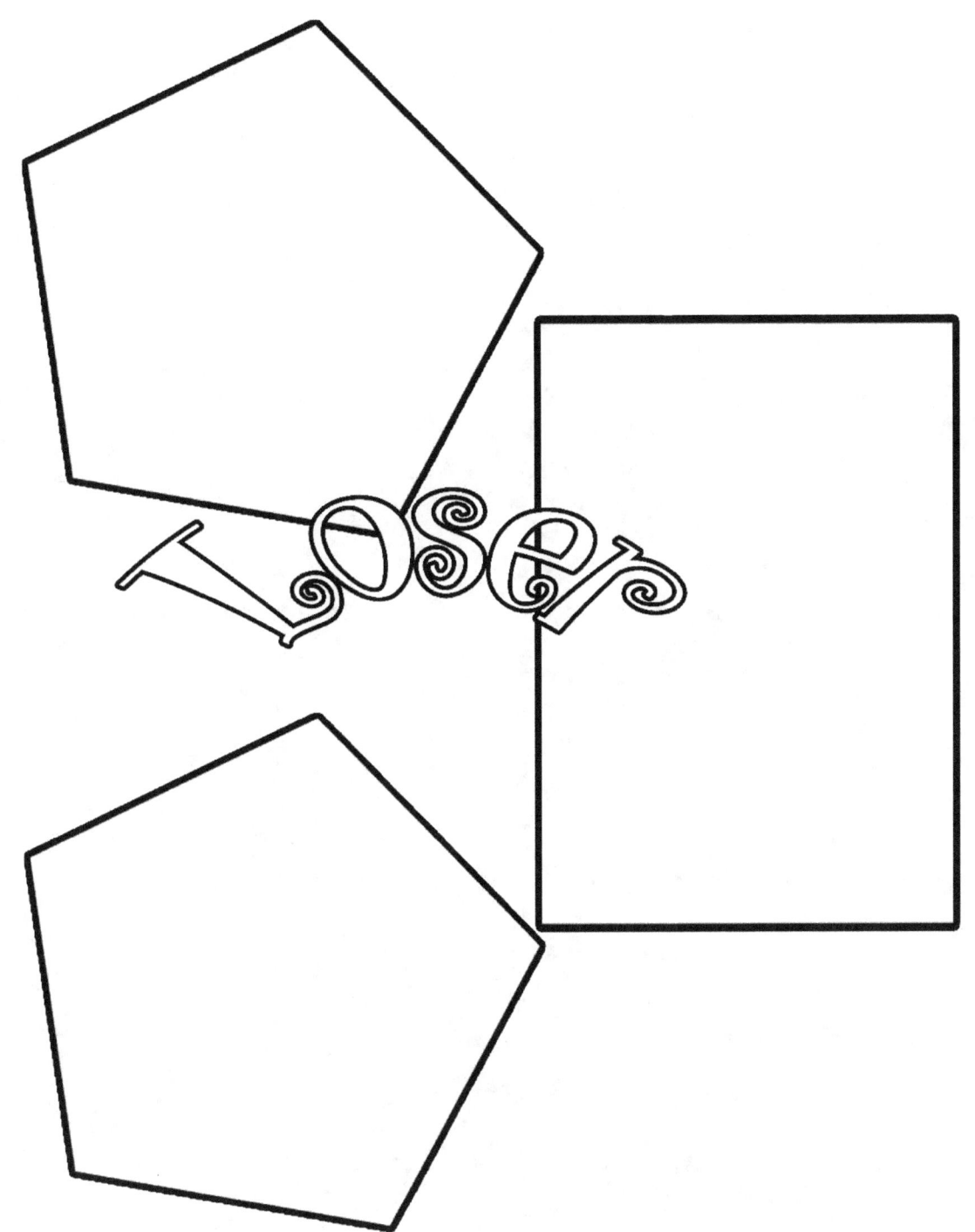

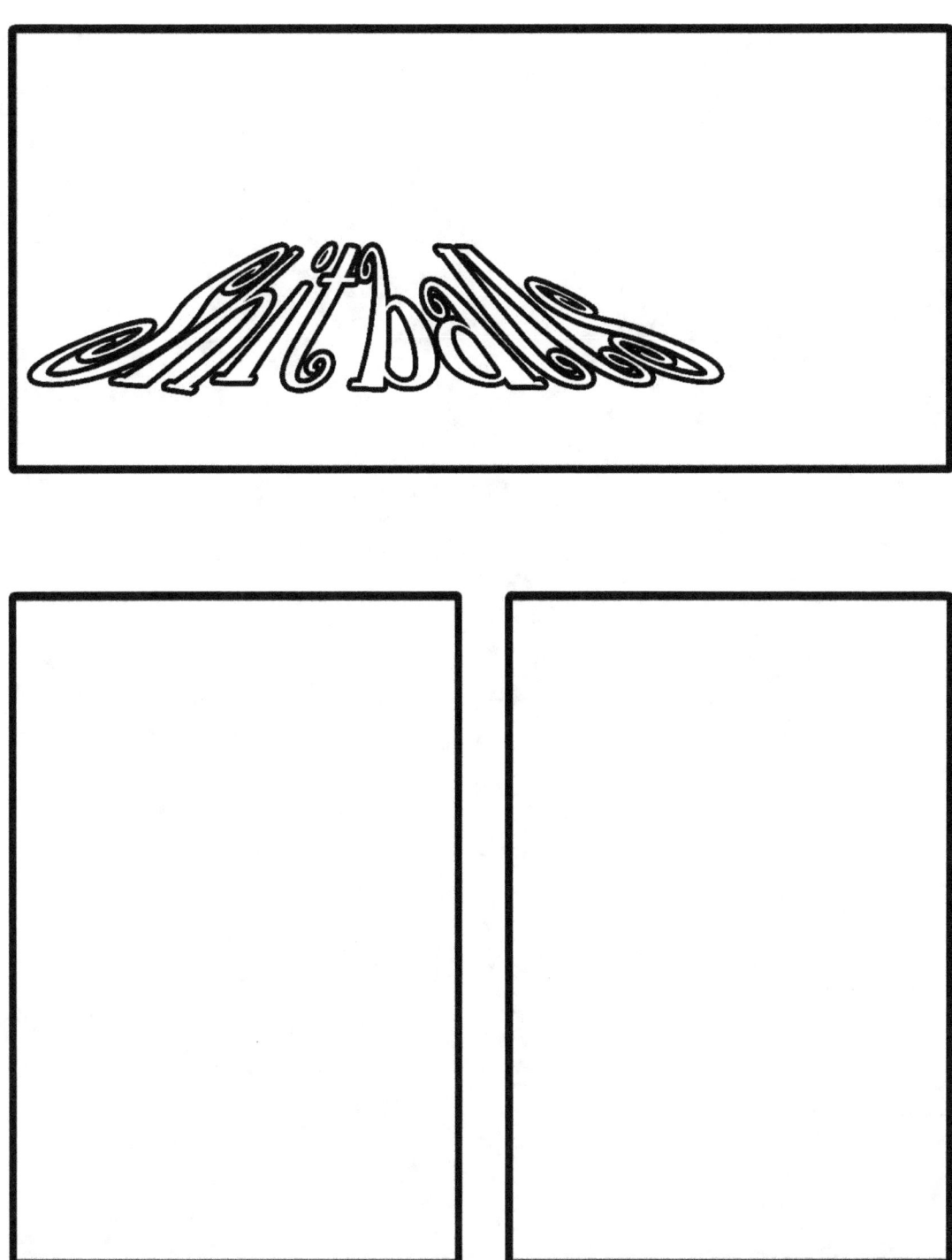

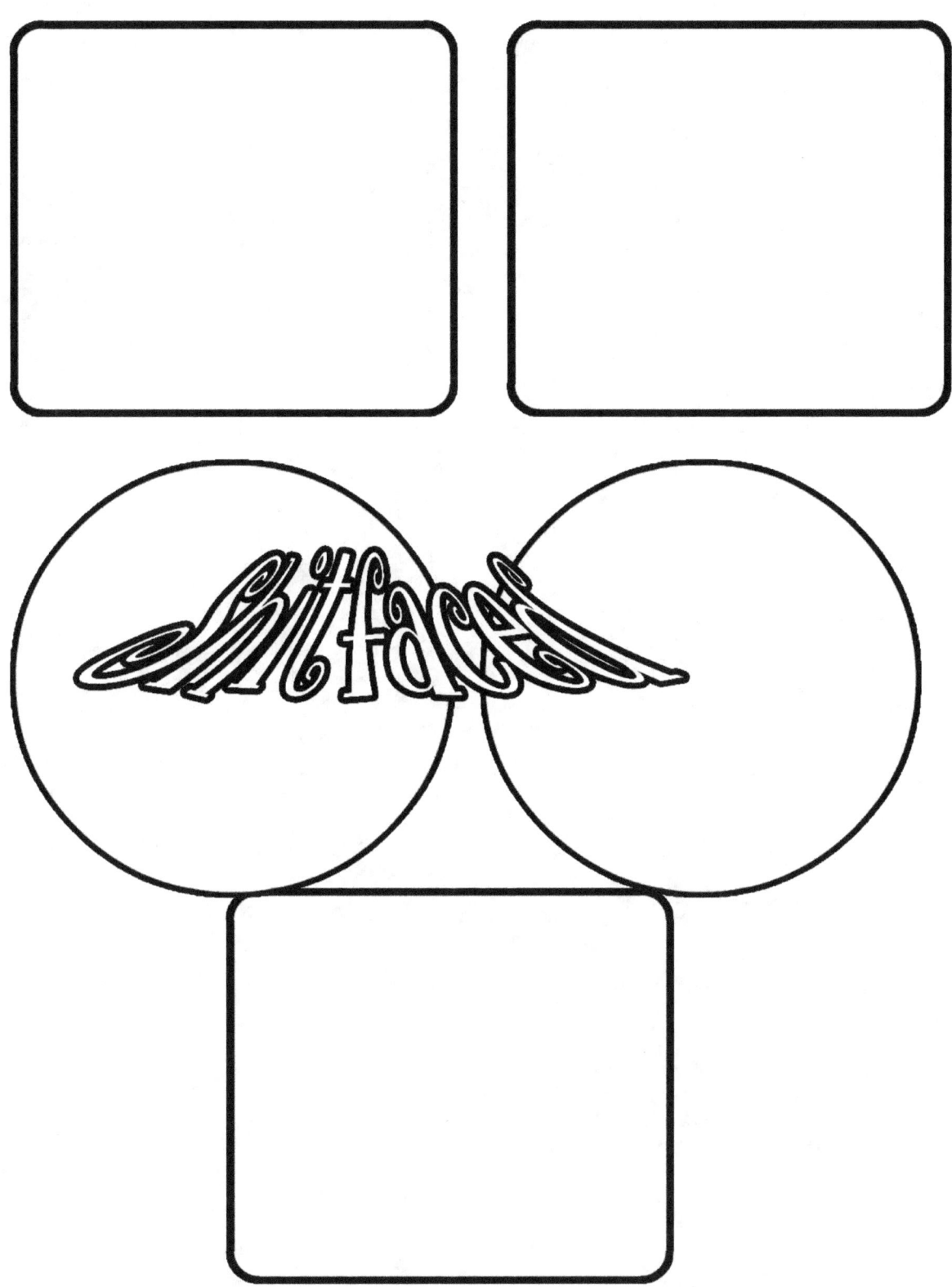

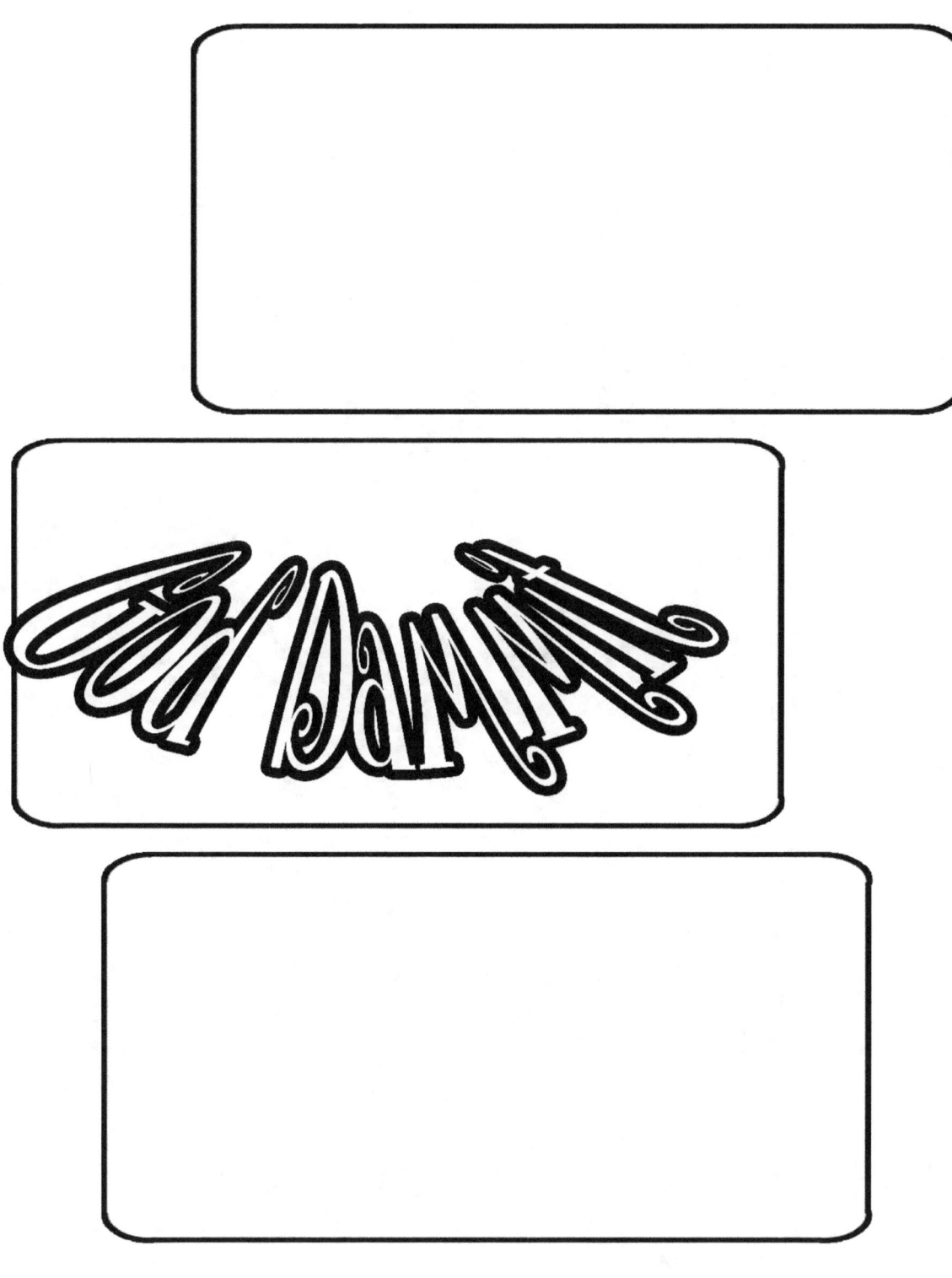

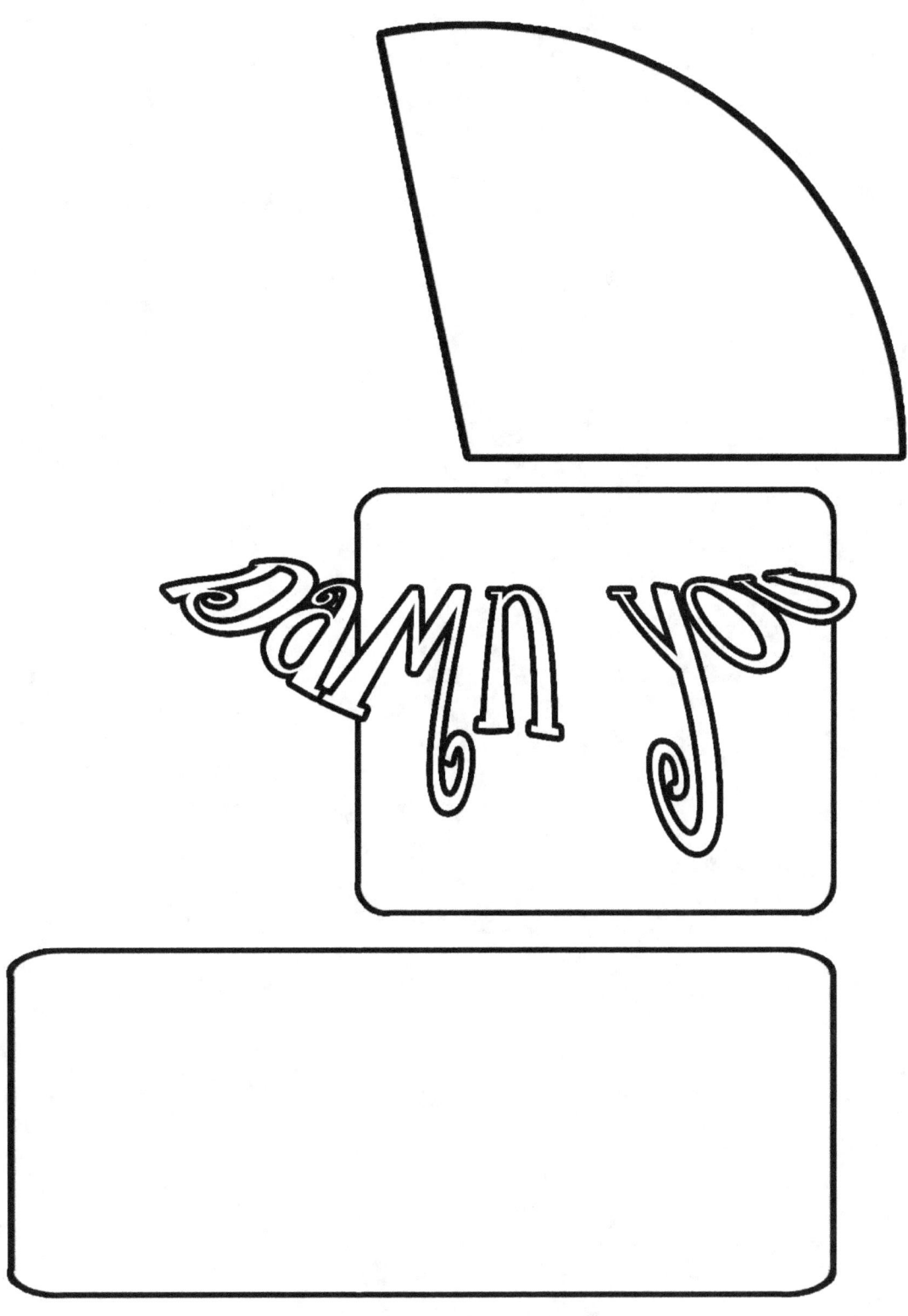

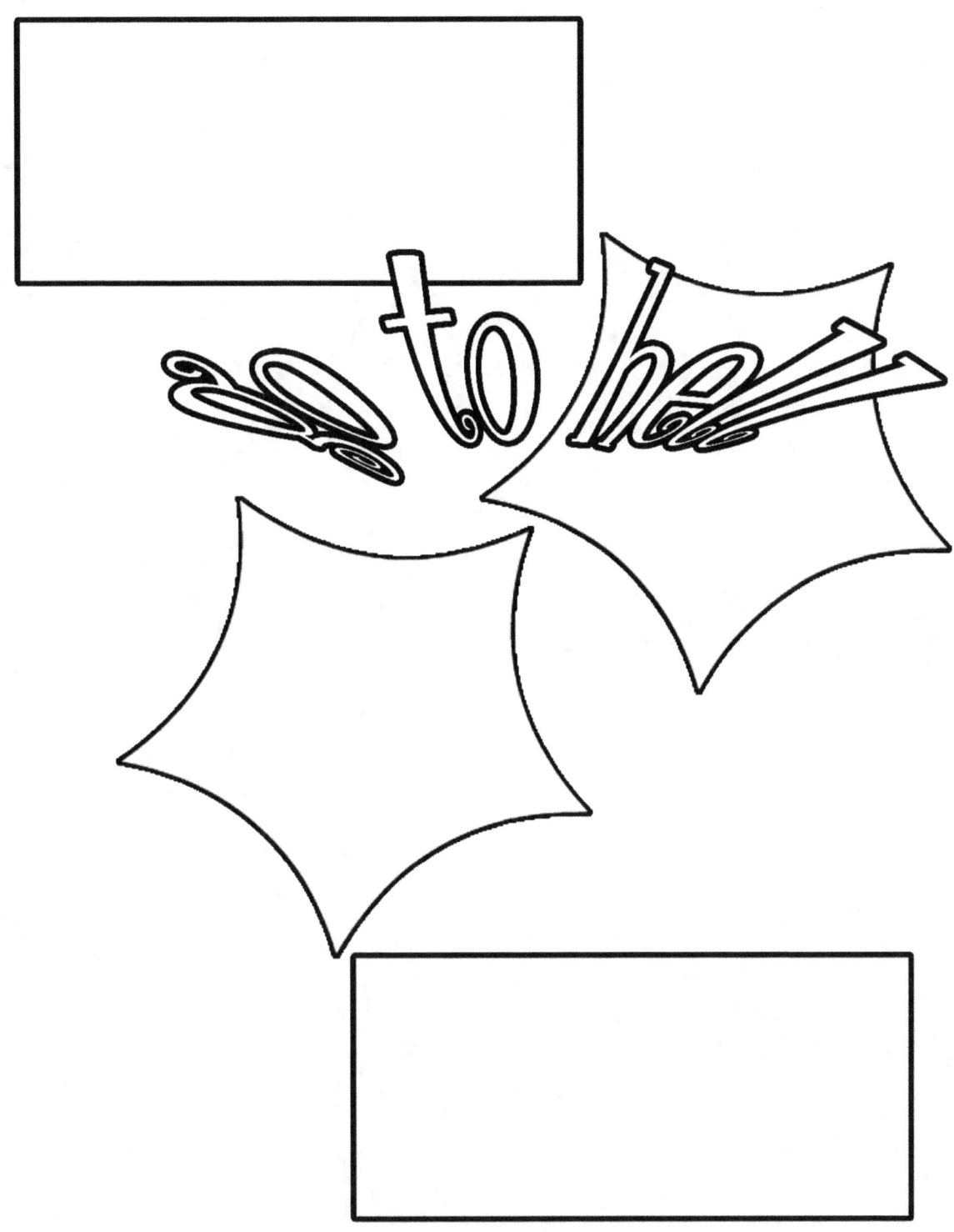

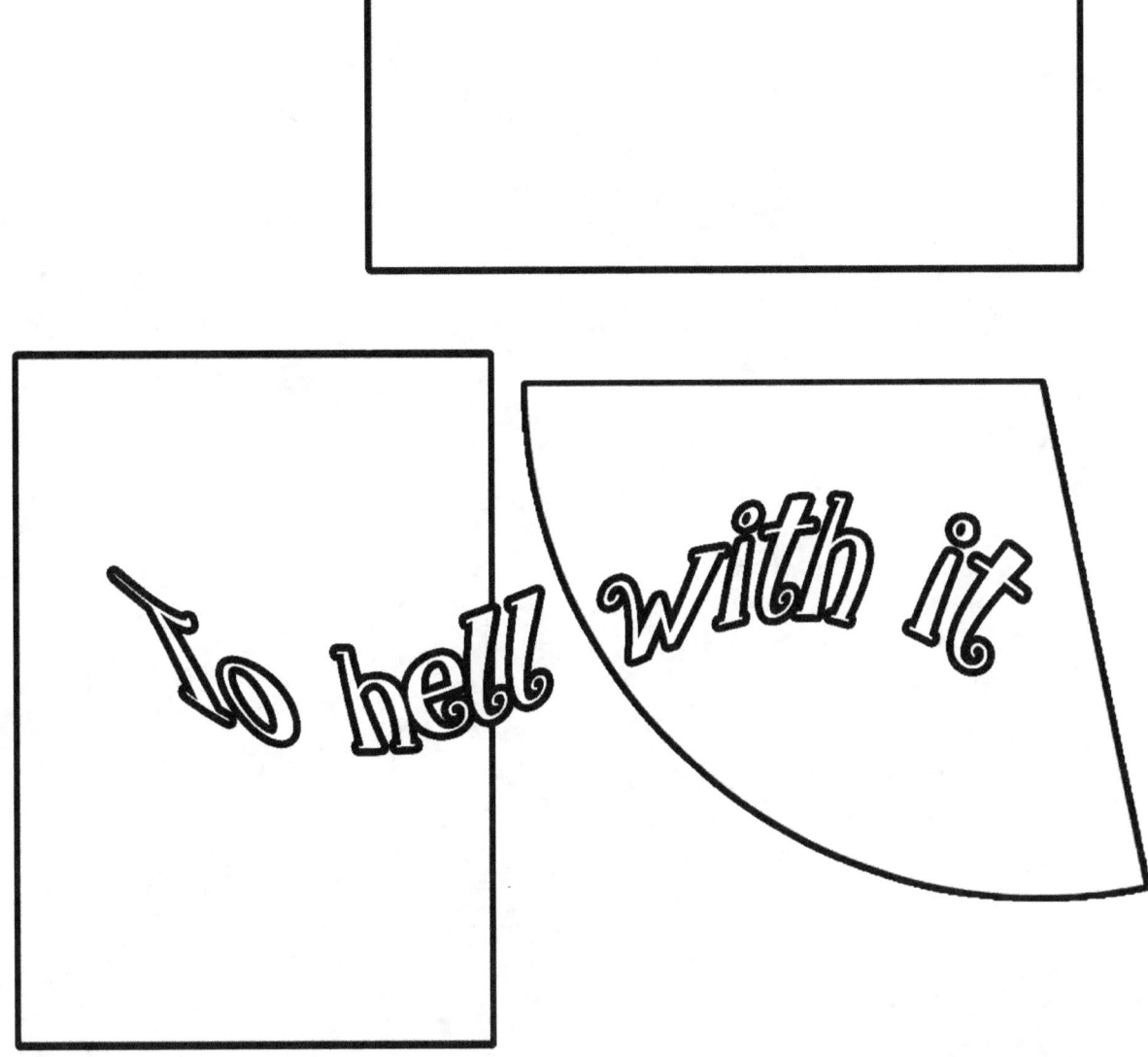

What an hole

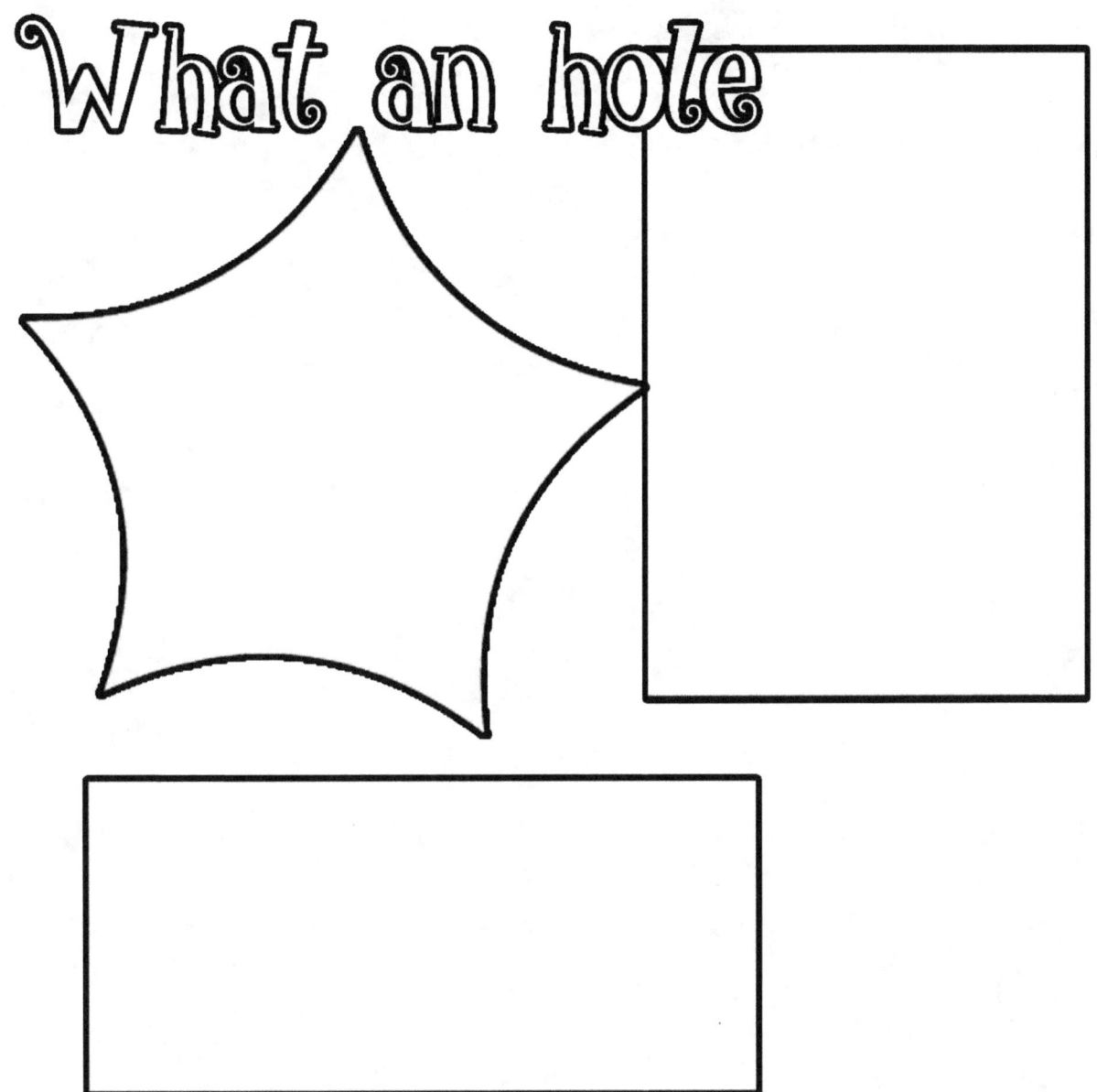

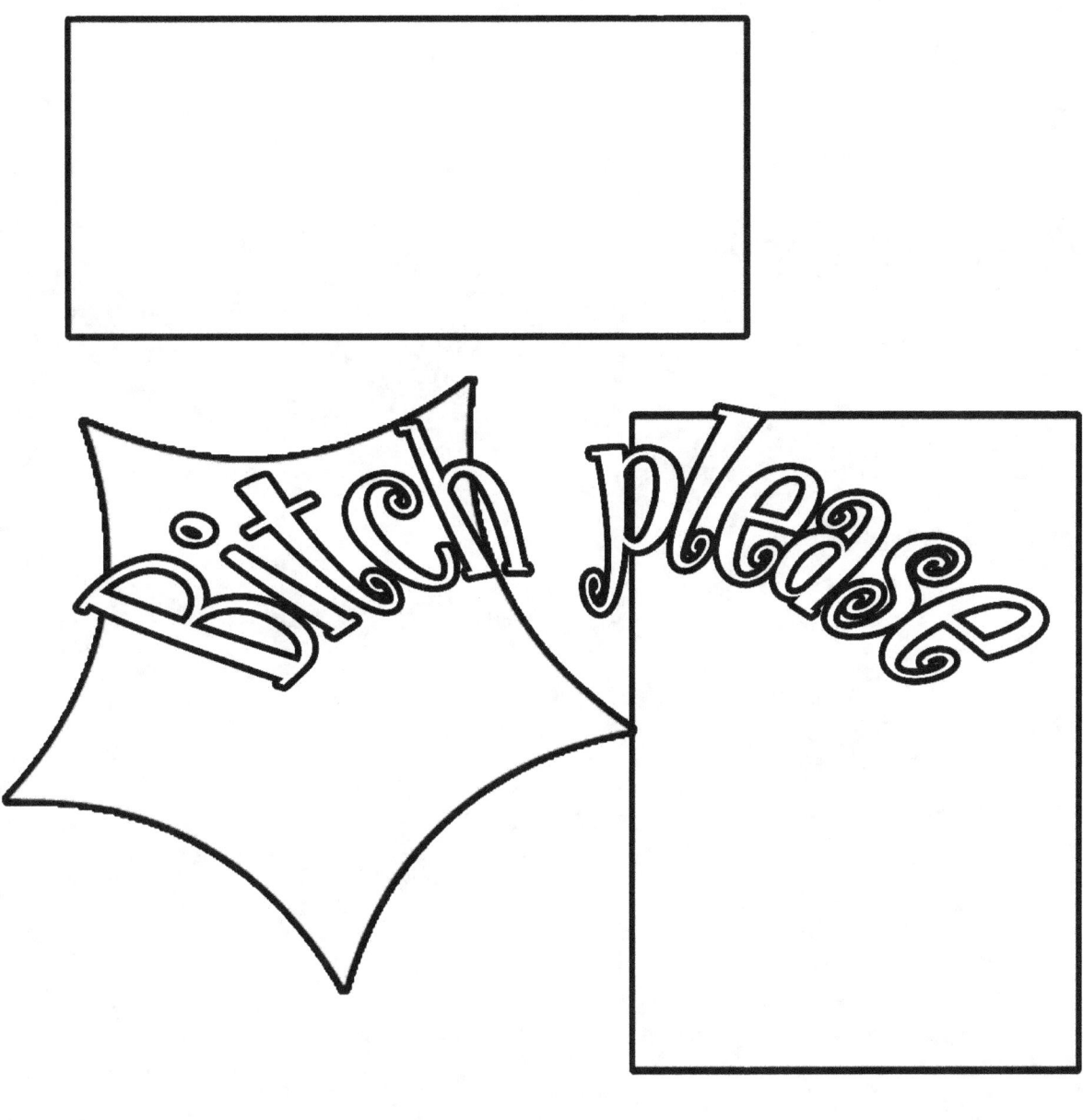

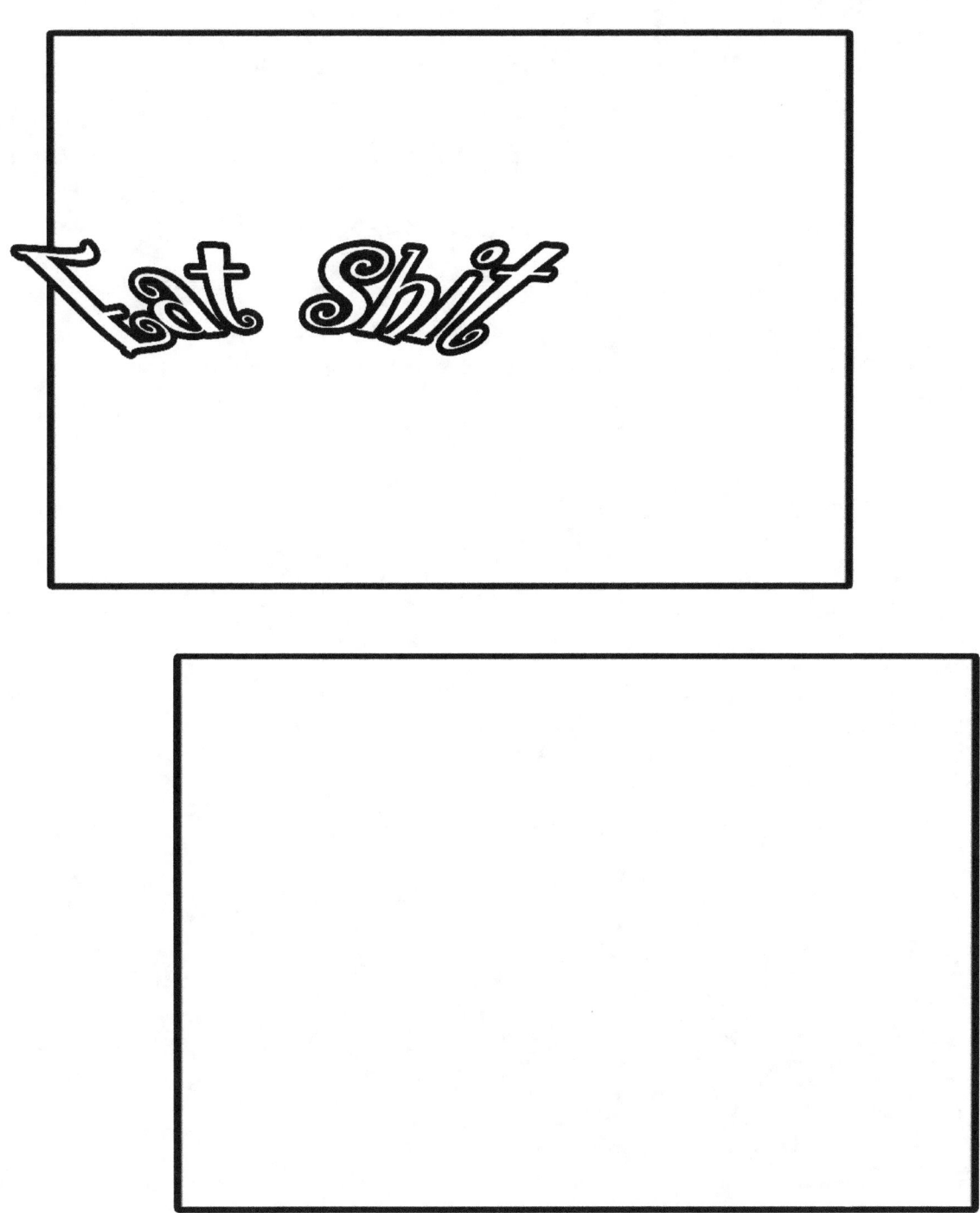

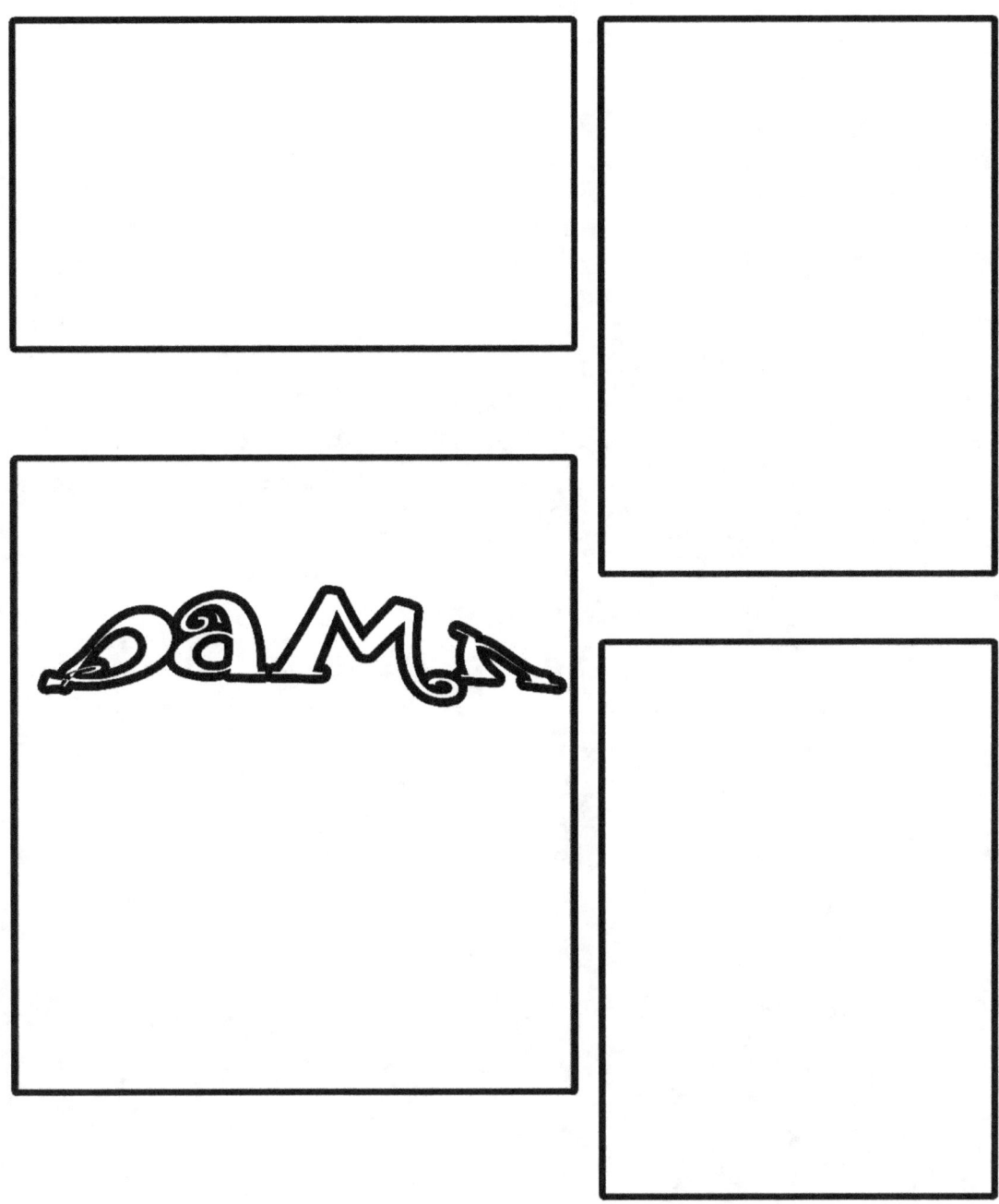

You are shit

Out of luck

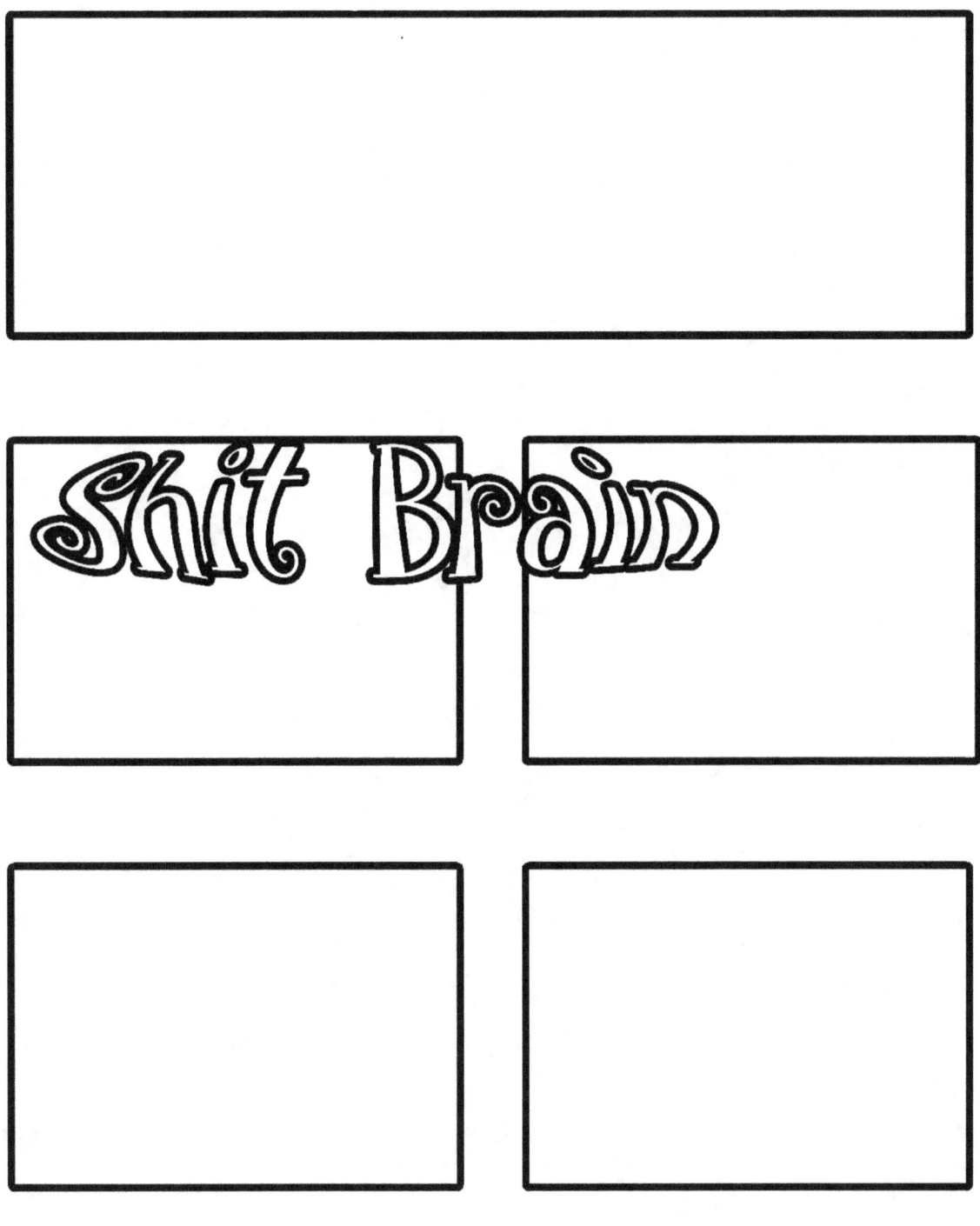

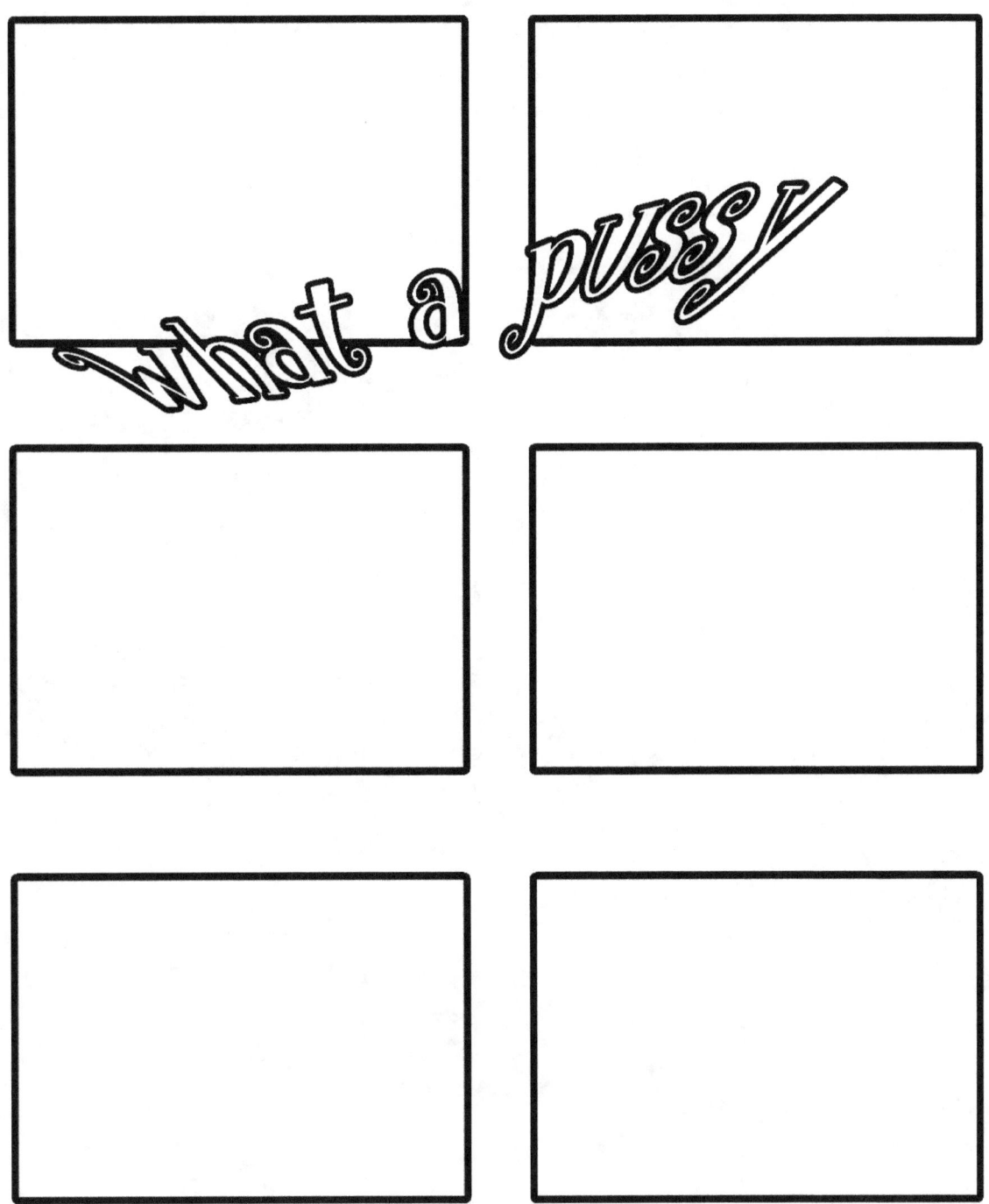

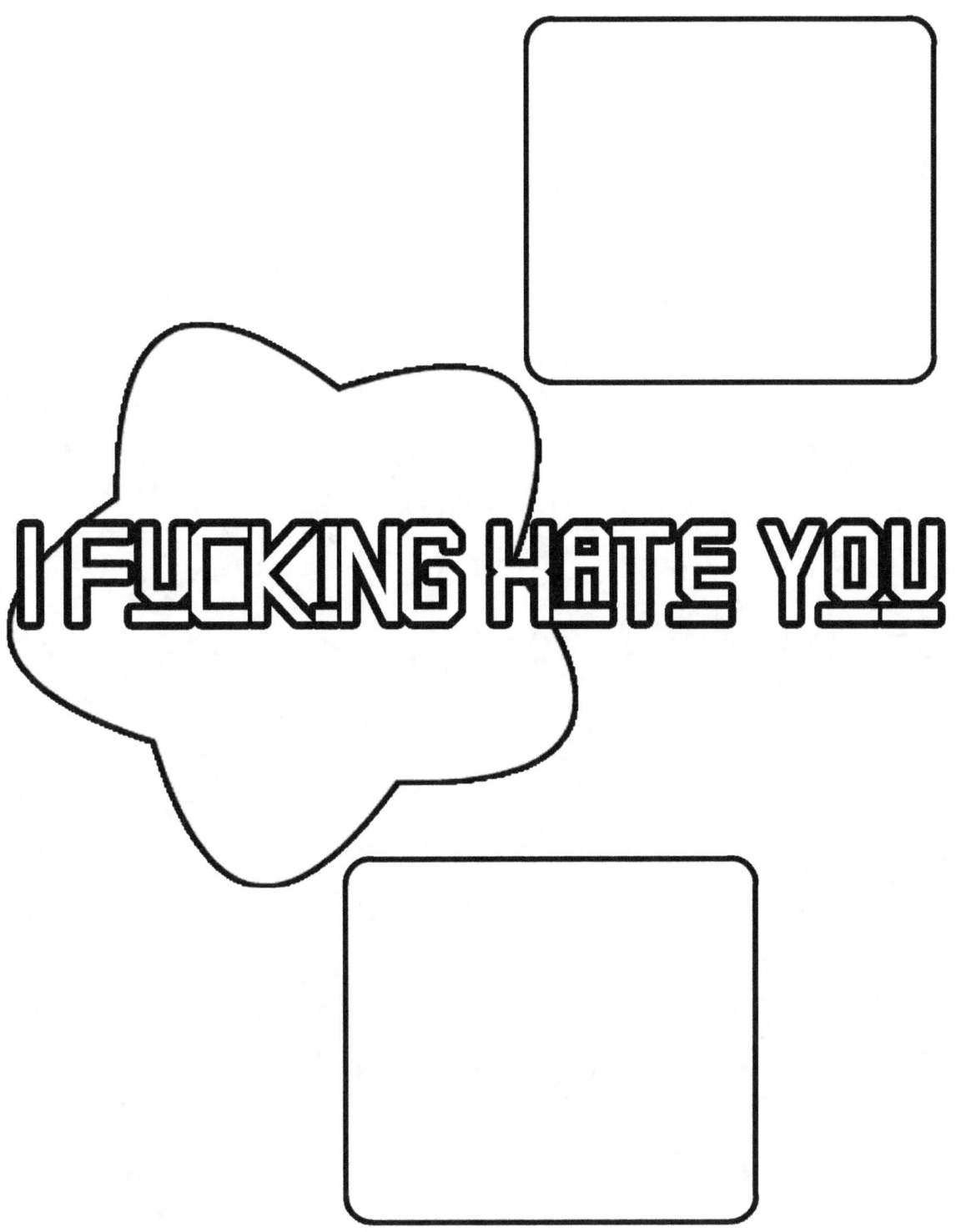

I FUCKING HATE YOU

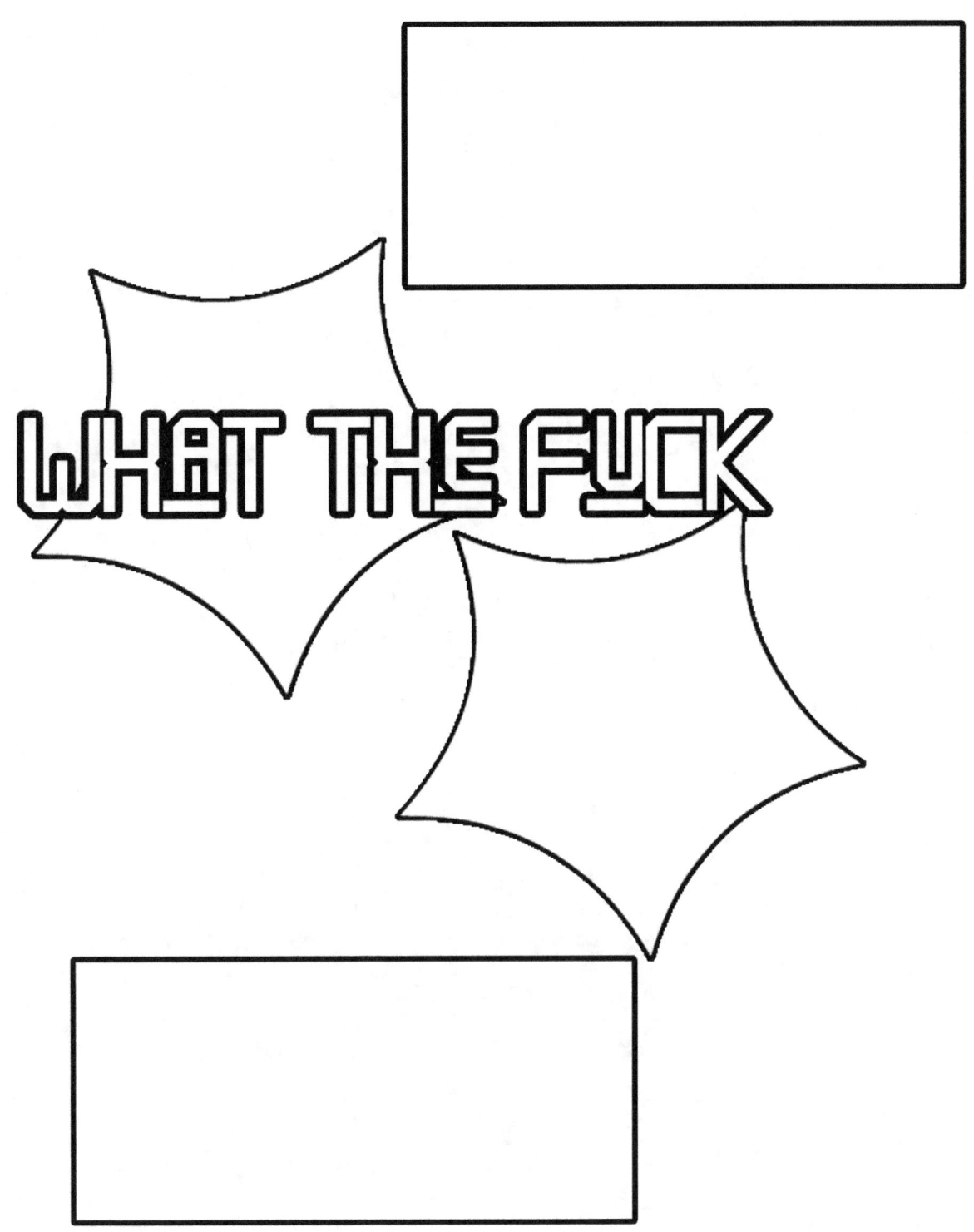

SON OF A B!TCH

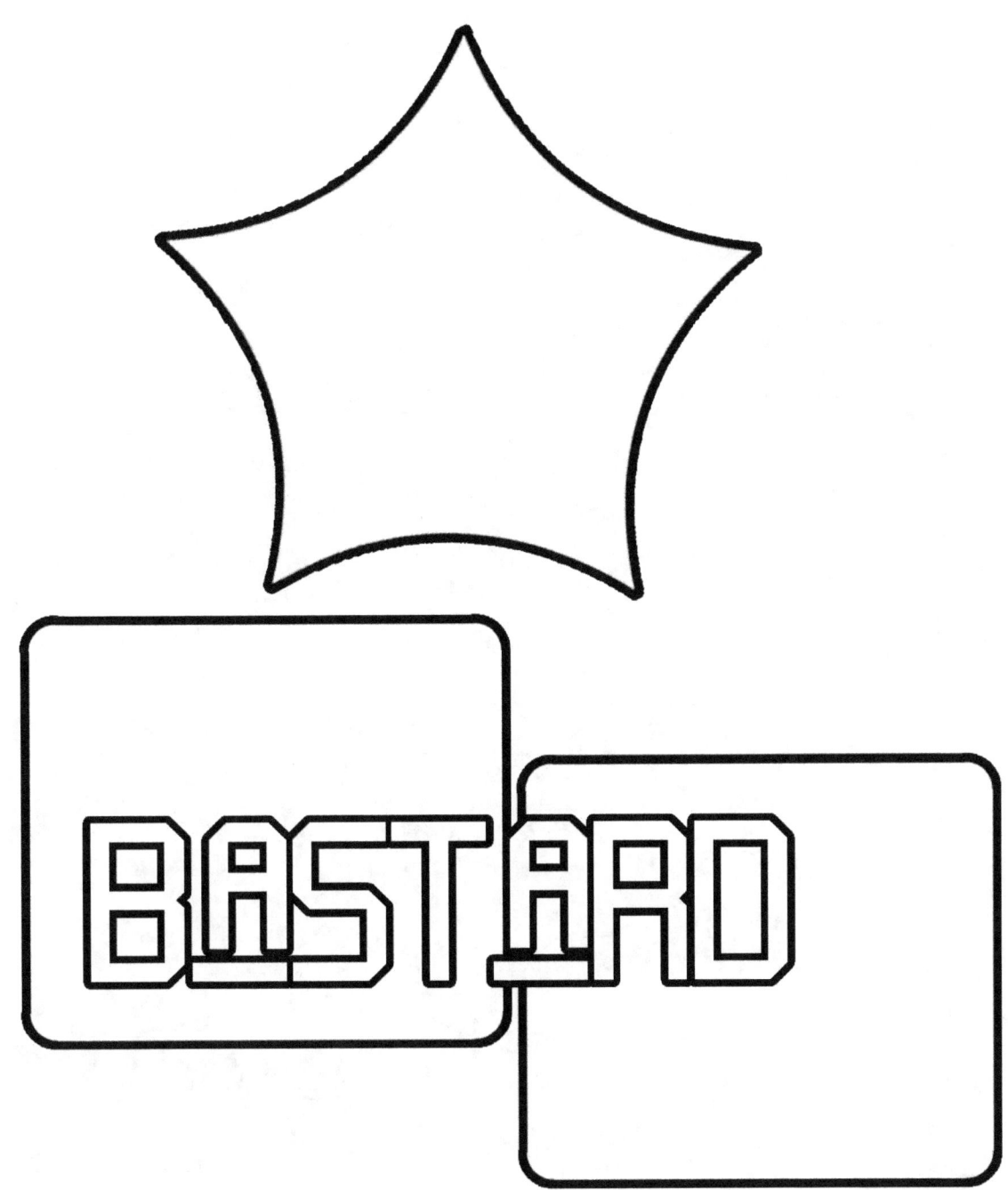

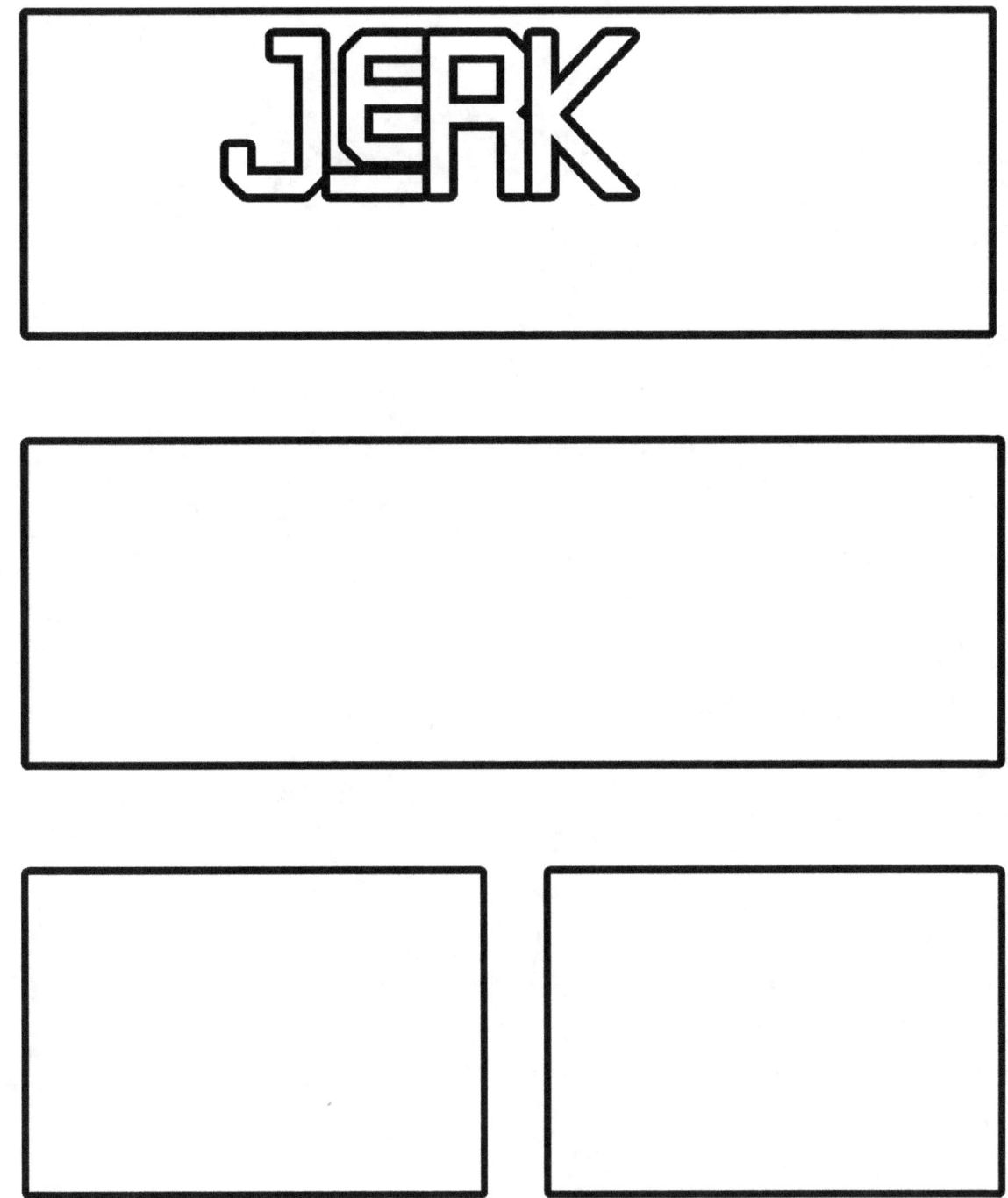

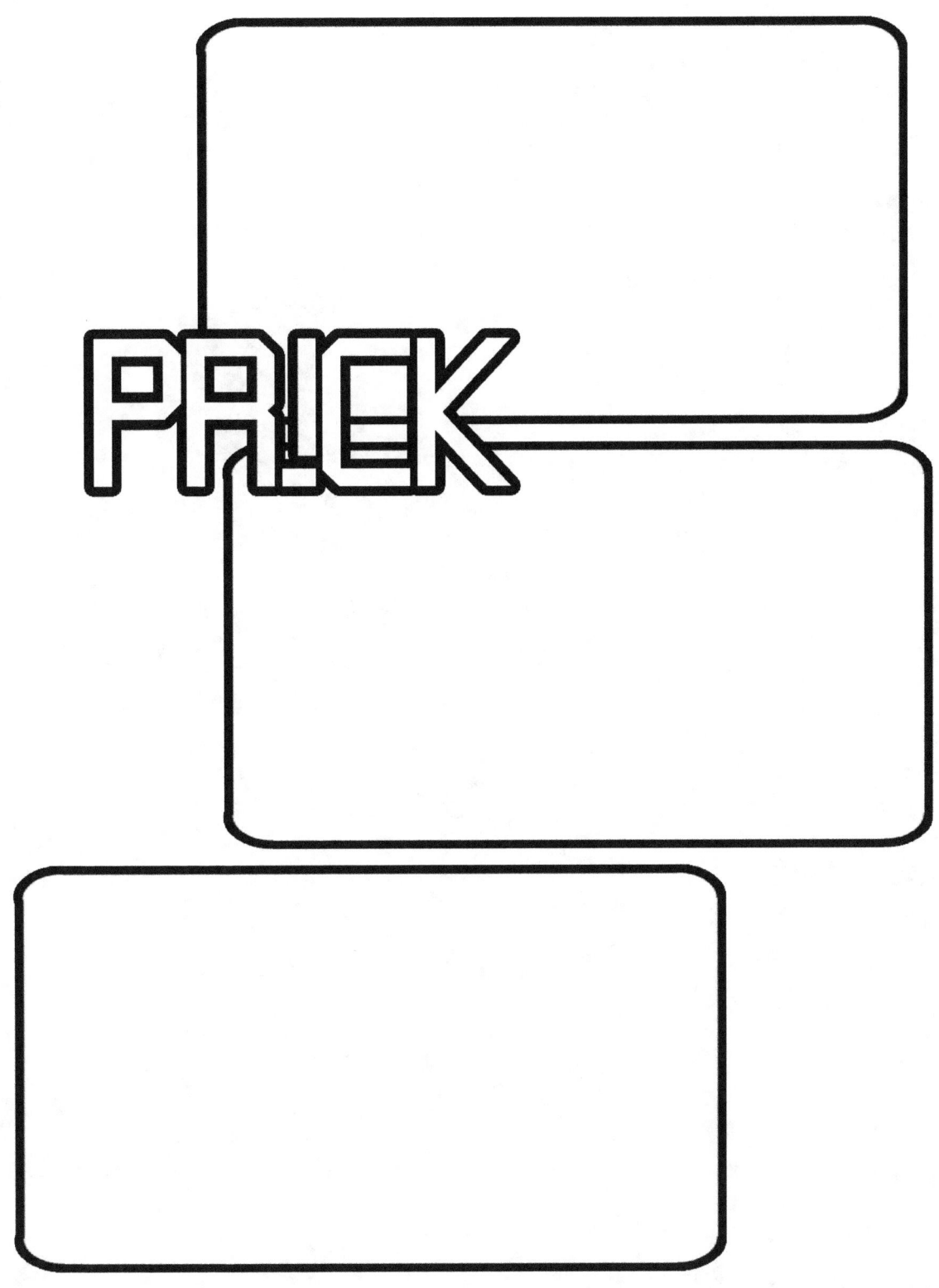